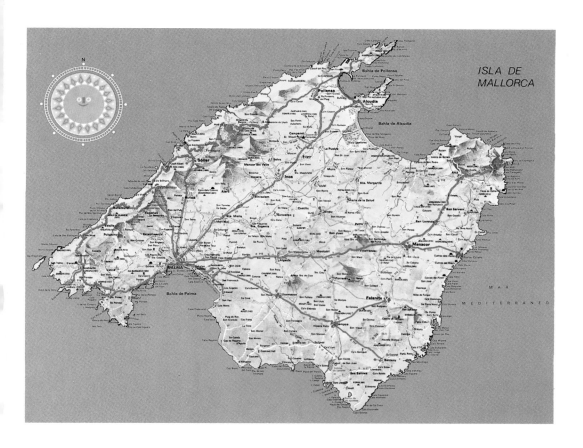

# Mallorca

Photographs:

Archivo Editorial REPRECO, C.B.

EDITADO POR:
REPRECO-CB
Cerdaña, 8, Entlo.
07012 PALMA DE MALLORCA
Tel. (971) 72 63 56

Edición 1997

ISBN 84-398-2812-8
Depósito legal B-24993-95
Printend in Spain - Impreso en España

Serper S.L., Sugrañes, 94 Tel. 298 15 00 -Barcelona

# THE ENCHANTMENT OF THE ISLAND

*Throughout these pages commenting on the different aspects of the Balearic Islands, in unison with the purely narrative parts, there are interspersed, perhaps with even greater attractive force, the marvellous landscapes picked out from among the beauties of Nature, that so prodigally sublimates the thousands of attractions that swarms of painters have managed to capture through their talent, and who never tire of proclaiming that they have found the Mecca of their dreams in the witchery of the Islands.*

*It is not our business here to underline the names fo artists, musicians and writers who, through the threads of their art, have succeeded in raising to the greatest height the name of the lovely Mediterranean Islands that enjoy a splendid history inherent in the development of a long series of civilizations. In a brief historical survey we come to realize to what extent the name of Majorca contributes in displaying to the world a whole gamut of genuine beauty that shares in the imperishable fame of that advanced geology of the Spanish peninsula towards the mysterious Orient.*

*The photographic lens has, with the modern colour technique, been able to fix the moments of the state of mind of the person holding the camera and raise the results obtained to the dignity of a Work of Art. Thus, he who has seen with his own eyes the emerald sea with its bed of pale sand and swaying seaweed, the blue sky furrowed with white and pink clous, and the cismontane little houses set like jewels on different planes of the island structure, may keep and renew the emotion he felt before the real and tangible vision on turning over the pages of this book when he is back from his visit any of the Isles.*

*Majorca, the Greater Balearic Island, with its harmonious proportions that enable it to enclose a number of more important towns and more than sixty villages situated in the mountains or on the plains; makes up, a fabulous sight that lulls the senses and leaves the soul in suspense.*

*The monuments of Palma, built of noble stone, — Bellver Castle, the Lonja (Exchange), the Cathedral with the Gotich lacework of its delicate architecture; — are indestructible elements joining the landscape to the sea, that modern iconoclastic ideas will never succeed in wiping out, since they are immanent in the Isle of Kindness and Beauty.*

*In the achieving of the aims of the editors of this book, perhaps the poetical contagion wich which the author of the*

*following lines endeavours to crown this prologue — devotep*
*to his beloved little Motherland Majorca —, may collaborate:*

*Island of Peace in waters of Plenty,*
*Land of Harmony, Wealth, and of Sun,*
*Country of pearl where Hope doth rest,*
*Refuge of Poetry and Love.*

*Temple where Mildness is worshipped,*
*Emporium of Beauty and Chivarly,*
*Garden where Praise is cultivated*
*of standards that for ever will last.*

*Mirror a thousand colours reflecting*
*Beneath the bright canopy of an open sky,*
*A host of great deeds in History.*

*With the almond in blossom, — a basket of flovers*
*Floating on the sea to the open world, —*
*Majorca — the vestibule of Glory.*

**Antonio Carlos VIDAL-ISERN**

Professor at the
«Real Academia de Ciencias Morales y Políticas»
Member of the
«Asociación Española de Escritores de Turismo»

«Dear Friends and Readers, if you are or imagine you are a victim of neurasthenia, deafened and confused by the noise of our modern civilization and the urge to arrive more quickly at some place where you have nothing to do, and if business has filled with numbers the space in your brain that is intended for what we call intelligence; if the cinema has damaged your optic organism, and the flickering has become chronic, and restlessness and worry will not let you live, and you want to enjoy a little of the rest to which anybody in this world is entitled who has done no harm to anyone, — then follow me to an island where calm always reigns and men are never in a hurry, where the women never grow old, where words are not wasted, where the sun stays longer than anywhere else and the Lady Moon moves more slowly, sleepy whith idleness.

This island, dear Readers, is Majorca.»

Thus spake Santiago Rusiñol, who was well up in poetic sayings and exact descriptions. We have not a more beautiful reference nor a better introduction to this book than the first words of «The Isle of Calm», where Majorca is described with love, where its spirit is sought out and, when found, becomes one with «waiting for the boat», whilst the sun's warmth invades the soul with a placid laziness.

We could go on quoting and illustrating our photos with his sayings but for the fear that «his» Majorca would not be precisely that of our days, that that legendary idleness is not already feeling the shock of a more throbbing life, that those solitary streets of Old Palma — «that echo like musical boxes marking the tempo of the footsteps, the sighs of the rocking cradle» — are already too far off to be the same lonely streets.

Majorca, Ibiza, the whole archipelago has come to live its new mission of infecting the world with its calm and sharing its treasures with the rest of the Universe. Statistics show fabulous figures of the traffic on its airports. The gilded blue-girdled land receives the great ones of the world as well as the more modest travelers. It can put them all up and put its seal on all of them, offer them landscapes and beauty, sun, sea and calm.

The Balearic Islands comprise — besides Majorca and Minorca — Ibiza the White, Formentera, Cabrera and a whole series of islets sprouting from the sea near the coast. There is Dragonera at the western point of Majorca, that offers to those arriving by boat the beautiful perspective of its rocky cliffs — a foretaste of the dazzling sight of the Bay of Palma, a few miles farther on —; the Isla del Aire off the coast of Minorca; Conejera near Ibiza, and Espalmador close to Formentera.

On the arrival of Spring, Majorca becomes covered all over with the white of her almonds, whose young blossoms rock with their murmurs the sleep of the tortured, ancient olive trees. The island is always in bloom because there is hardly any winter.

The Majorcan has slept in peace for only a few centuries. Although his origins are lost or but hazily perceived in the history of invasions, the chronicles describe him as a fighter. He was a master slinger who carried three slings into battle, — one in his hand, another tied to his head, and a third wound round his waist. It was said that no helmet could resist the force of the stones or balls that he used as shot. He took an active part in the struggles between Rome and Carthago, and it was the Roman general Quintus Cecilius Metellus who, after capturing the «Minor» island — our Minorca, landed on the «Major» one in 123 B.C. and founded Pollentia and Palma.

Vandals, Visigoths, Moors, and Aragonese Catalans fought for the island and captured it in turn. It was planted through the long years of Mohammedan domination with pomegranates and african palm-trees.

Bellver Castle, built by order of Jaime II., the son of the Conqueror, stands in front of the bay like a symbol of the years when Majorca was an independent kingdom with a flourishing trade around the Mediterranean.

Since the national union the history of the islands has been merged with that of Spain, and the Majorcan — contented in the peace of his island — has been forging that calm and carefree character, philosophically enjoying the beauty of everything in Majorca and the other islands of the archipelago that — as they say — came up from the sea for a sun-lounge, and they liked it so much that they fell asleep and stayed there.

# Mallorca

Night over the Bay

Palma embraces the sea and holds it within the marvellous setting of its bay. All kinds of light and all colours seem to have arranged to meet here. Blazing clouds glow there in the evening, whilst — at the same time — the sails of the boats in the harbour, the great hotels, the pine groves, the palm-trees, the Cathedral, and Bellver Castle are mirrored in the limpid water.

The Promenades and Gardens project out into the sea. As there is so much sea, the City can please itself by raising more and more buildings at its edge, and never coming to an end. Palma is becoming modern without losing its personality. The vanes of the windmills in the Jonquet group seem to be illuminated, so near are the impressive groups of modern buildings.

From the Sagrera Promenade, seated in the shade of the palm-trees, one has a full view of the harbour. In this sunny and gay palm-lined avenue, we see the monument to Rubén Darío, the «Consulado del Mar» (Maritime Consulate), and the very beautiful Gothic monument that is the Lonja or Exchange, built in 1426 by the architect after whom the avenue is named, — Guillermo Sagrera. The tympanum of the principal entrance is decorated with an angel that reminds one of those that adorn French cathedrals of the same period. The outside seems to have been gilded by the sun and burned by the saltpeter from the sea. In the interior the pillars are shaped like tree trunks, and their veins, spreading out to support the arch, give them the appearance of stone palm-trees. Today, the Lonja has lost its commercial character, and its sole hall shelters the Fine Arts Gallery.

Paseo Sagrera

S'Hort del Rei

The Shipyard, the Lonja and the trees in Sagrera Promenade frame the ever-outstanding silhouette of the Cathedral. Its structure, massive and bristling with towers and buttresses, is like — at one and the same time — a temple, a fortress and another rock among the cliffs. It is reflected in the sea which, robbing it of its rigidity, rocks it as if Palma had two cathedrals, — one between heaven and earth, the hieratic one, and the other shimmering in the sea. Behind the Avenue, the very popular Santa Catalina quarter seethes, where some excellent restaurants have been opened.

Palacio Marqués Vivot

Maritime Promenade gardens and Cathedral

Marine Park.

The Cathedral.

S'Arenal

Ca'n Pastilla

Cala Estancia

Cala Gamba

Ciutat Jardí

Portitxol

Palma de Mallorca

Porto Pi

Castell
de Bellver

Cala Major

Ca's Cat

Corner of the Harbour. Background : The Cathedral

etes

Portals Nous

Palmanova

Magaluf

The palaces and mansions abound in the old quarter of
the City, near the Cathedral, the church of Santa Eulalia
and Born Avenue. They preserve their fine Majorcan fur-
niture as treasures. Their typical features are the magni-
ficent inner courtyards, full of light and peace, and that
may be seen from the front gate. Among these palaces
we must mention the Oleza, Morell, Ferradell, Berga, Des-

A flash of the Bay

Almudaina Palace

Bullfight Ring

Plaza de la Reina

Paseo Marítimo

Paseo Sagrera

27

S'Arenal

S'Arenal

puig, Pueyo, Desbrull, Montenegro, and that of Vivor whose harmonious courtyard we illustrate.

All the ruggedness of Palma Cathedral front, however, conceals the light and softness of the interior. Its stained-glass windows cast rainbows of light between the powerful pillars. The building of the Cathedral lasted from 1230 until the XVII. century, and the Gothic of its design shows later touching up. And Gaudi still represents in it the art of our epoch. The remains of the two great monarchs of Majorca — Jaime II. and Jaime III. — are kept here in Trinity Chapel.

In the evening, Palma Bay is bathed in an infinite peace, and the night mirrors in its waters the thousand lights that preside over the imposing shadow of Bellver Castle. Sagrera Avenue — that joins the Maritime Promenade — leads to the tourist and residential district, peopled mainly by

S'Arenal

Ca'n Pastilla

artists and foreigners. Porto Pi, Son Armadans, El Terreno, patches of golden land between two blue elements; little white houses among flowers and woods, with the aroma of pine trees and sea, shine at night with the fire of all the stars in the Universe.

The Castle is the most treasured ornament of Majorca, and Majorca is the most beautiful jewel of the Castle, for if it is worth the trouble of climbing the hill to visit the Museum, it is worth a thousand times more effort solely to enjoy the view from there. The bay, the town and its surroundings, the harbour, the Cathedral, the sea and the sky, all bathed in the golden light of certain evenings when the sunset is vastly more beautiful than would be possible anywhere else.

At the foot of the Castle lies Gomila Place and the cosmopolitan district of Son Armadans.

Cala Mayor

Palma is a town full of contrasts. Next door to the modern layout and the luxurious buildings in the Plaza de la Reina, exquisite fruit and vegetables of Majorcan produce are set out for sale. Beside the gay colours of the bull-ring, the no less colourful harbour — full of life and movement, with shipping from all the seven seas — is to be seen. The predominant elements are the promenades, the palm groves and the sun-gilded sea.

When we look out from the Cathedral belvedere, we see the bay and on our left the new urbanizations, the beaches and hotels of S'Arenal, Maravillas, Coll d'en Rabassa, Can Pastilla, and the Garden City. On our right we have Corp Mari, El Terreno, San Augustín, Cala Mayor, Cas Catalá, Ses Illetes, Portals Nous... Each has its own special atmosphere and its particular countryside, so much so that we seem to be miles removed from the capital of what is nothing other than a splendid prolongation. The broad curve of Palm Bay — $13^1/_2$ miles across from Cala Figuera to Cap Blanc — shelters them all in its enormous cockle-shell whose cragged verdant banks possess a cove, a beach corner or a little harbour for each of them. Thus, there are — between rocks and pines — Portals Nous, Punta Negra, Palma Nova, Magaluf, and the lovely creek of Bendinat.

Cala Mayor is the result of a successful blending of the business and tourist element with loyalty to nature. It is a broad protected beach only 4 miles from Palma. Among the pine tress there spring up hotels offering all modern comfort, and it is not only beautiful in itself but is a splendid starting point for excursions. At night, the whole of Cala Mayor is reflected in the still waters of the cove, transformed into a swaying mass of lights.

San Agustin

Illetes

Not far from Palma, three crags floating apparently on the surface of the water give the name to «Ses Illetes». Their transparent waters reflect the pine trees, for whose tips swimmers seem to be diving.

The road is always careful not to go away from the sea. It runs alongside it and, if it leaves it for a few hundred yards, it is to come out again in front of it. When the eye follows it, it is visible all the time, opening or bending round the little creeks perfumed by the intense Majorcan vegetation — lavender, thyme, broom —.

The coves nearest to Palma have witnessed the erection of a splendid group of hotels. Residences, restaurants and hotels line the coast and attract an infinite number of Spanish and foreign tourists throughout a season that scarcely ends even in winter. Ships and planes land thousands who intend to spend their holidays on the Island. In summer, Son San Juan airport is one of those that show the largest tourist traffic in the world. And so, Majorca is once more invaded, but it is a peaceful invasion of those seeking sun and sea, and who come to dream with their eyes open, stretched out on the warm sands of her beaches.

Illetes

Majorca has the music of the sea, the murmuring of the wind in the trees, the warm light of the sun by day. Her nights sing rhythmic «boleros» or hum in silence. There is also the strident music of the restaurants in modern jazz

Illetes

time that enlivens and entertains those who like this kind
of entertainment, with drinking, dancing and laughing with
the ephemeral merriment of the holidays that makes friend-
ships in a few hours. New attractions and fresh forms
and colours have appeared in the landscape; the blue,
green, yellow or red spots of the umbrellas, the thousand
shades of the bathers, and the gracefulness of the girls
resting and bronzing their skin in the sun.

Illetes

Portals Nous

Behind the crags after which it is named, Ses Illetes, its beach and its manors go to make up an extraordinarily beautiful spot, with excellent and comfortable hotels. Portals Nous is only 6 $\frac{1}{2}$ miles from Palma; Palma Nova and Magaluf are 8 and 9 miles, respectively. Thanks to the prodigy of the Balearic climate, they are cool in summer and warm in winter.

Palma Nova is one of the most spacious and ambitious among the urbanized places on the Island. It too, has — like Cala Mayor — a large beach with pine trees coming down to the water-side. It is surrounded by hills and is a favourite summer resort of the inhabitants of Palma.

Majorca has such a lot of sea that there is always enough for the visitor to feel he has a little corner of shore for himself, and a bit of sea of his own. «It is a more Latin Island than all the others, — a land where one may rest

Palma Nova

Palma Nova

Magaluf

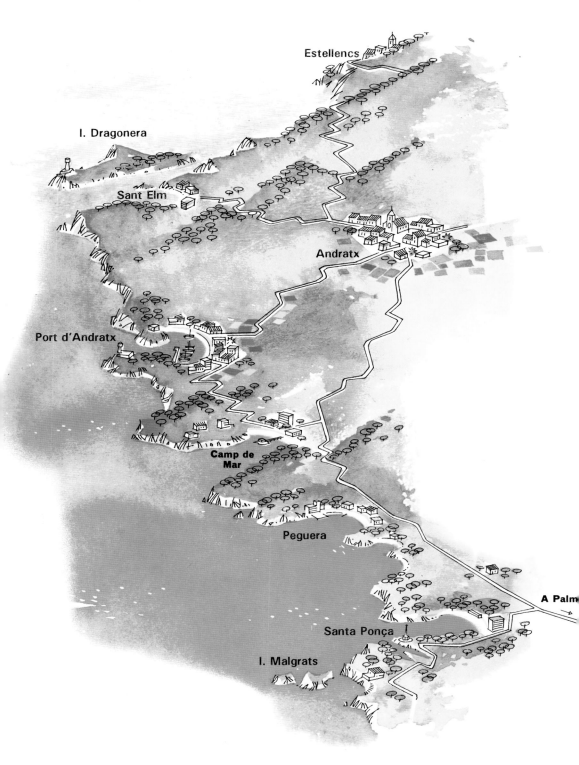

Estellencs

I. Dragonera

Sant Elm

Andratx

Port d'Andratx

Camp de Mar

Peguera

A Palm

Santa Ponça

I. Malgrats

40

and dream awake», said Santiago Rusiñol. And universal, though Latin, Majorca has learned to speak all cultured languages to greet and attend to her guests.

The road from Palma to Andraitx glides through splendid landscapes in which those who cross them will stop their car a hundred times to enjoy the panoramas offered them. Once we have left Palma Nova behind, Majorca's medieval history begins to show its reminiscences.

A little oratory marks the place where the first Mass was said on the Island, when the Catalan conquerors arrivesd in the land at the order of King Jaime I. In the Santa Ponsa Creek, a slender white cross tells us that here the great

Mirador d'es Malgrats

Santa Ponça

King landed, and commemorates the great expedition.

Between Penya and Santa Ponsa Coves, the Malgrat islands, craggy and majestic, are of impressive beauty. Then come the coves of Paguera, Fornells, and Camp de Mar, with their rugged outlines and transparent water, considered to be the most interesting to visitors in the whole Island. Branch roads lead to them, and to the numerous «balconies» over immense tracts of land.

The route halts at the little sheltered harbour of Andraitx, which, until recently, was a refuge for fishing boats, unknown to the tourist. Andraitx, however, a little inland, is a splendid starting point for excursions. The roads are festooned along the coast. Here it is abrupt, with hardly any beaches, and its few coves shelter the fishermen when the sea is very rough. S'Arracó and the «balcony» of San Telmo that opens onto the bare rock of Dragonera — the watcher of the sea with the penetrating eye of its lighthouse — are indeed very beautiful.

From Andraitx, the road — sprinkled with belvederes — goes to Bañalbufar on the rocky North coast, and once again we must stop, because at this point each view is more lovely than the last, whichever way we look, and every one of them is well worth seeing for itself. The most outstand-

Santa Ponça

Santa Ponça

Peguera

Cala Fornells

Camp de Mar

ing and spectacular of the panoramas are the ones domi-
nated by the «balconies» of Ricardo Roca and El Mirador
de las Animas.

The road — winding in constant turnings and hairpin
bends — now takes us to a new corner of the Majorcan
Paradise, Valldemosa.

Valldemosa, situated at the foot of Mount Teix, lit up
with intense brown tones, exulting vermilions and flaming
ocre tints, is beyond doubt one of the most lovely places
in the Majorca countryside. The clean little hamlet with its
pleasant, shady streets, fine but discrete in style, inspires
a deep sense of peace and an elegant melancholy nostalgia.
The inhabitants live from the abundant produce of the
agriculture on this fertile soil, clothed with the most beautiful trees. In January and February, the almonds and cher-

ries are in bloom, covering the broad countryside with a light pinkish tint.

In 1872, the Archduke Louis Salvador of Austria increased the value of this country that had already known in Miramar the enlightening footsteps of Ramón Llull, and at whose feet there nestles the great crag of Sa Foradada, a rough piece of rock jutting out into the sea, and that is higher than the tower of Palma Cathedral. At its summit the water had bored an enormous hole that gives it its name, and sun and sea have lent it all imaginable colours.

The foreign visitor knows Valldemosa from its Monastery, because it had been the refuge of the amours of Frederic Chopin and Georges Sand. The Majorcans, however, know Valldemosa as the country of «their» little

Camp de Mar

Port d'Andratx

saint, Catalina Thomás, the sweet child who has an altar in every islander's heart, and whose uncorrupted body is preserved in Palma.

The sea-loving traveler stops but a short time in Valldemosa. He scarcely knows even the cells and the museum of the Carthusian Monastery at San Bruno, founded in 1399 by the pious Catalan King Martín the Humane, and that was erected in its present form by the monks in the XVIII. century. Climbing roses and wonderful geraniums cover the walls of the Monastery that stands out among a dense vegetation of cypresses, palms, orange and lemon trees. In the interior, lively reminiscences of the romantic pianist and the exalted authoress abound. From the cell windows the beautiful landscape stretches out as far as the pass, and from there to the great plain with the houses of Palma, the sea, and a small cloud level with the water.

Sant Elm

that is Cabrera, the desert island. «If it is Spring, the trees
will be in full bloom, and in Summer they will be so full
of fruit, that it is a marvel», says Rusiñol, who lived at Valldemosa, and wrote, among other pretty phrases, that it
was a village made only for land workers and painters; for
the former... to live on their fields that are so fresh and so
clean, that one might even say they washed the dust from
their tomato plants; and for the latter... to spend their lives
painting it.

So lived, too, the Archduke Louis Salvador, the Suredas,
the painter Muntaner, Rubén Darío, the painter Mir... Here
lives also the artist José Coll-Bardolet, who knew how to
paint the atmosphere of the Majorcan dances. He often
painted the folk dances of the local group «El Parado»,
conducted by Maestro Bartolomé Estarás.

On leaving Valldemosa we come to Miramar. Again the

La Dragonera

Estellencs

sea spreads out before us and — as we have not seen it for a little while — it now seems more sea and more immense because we are seeing it from above. Once again we remember the poet's words, when he tells us that there was once a little boy on this island, who would not bathe because he was afraid he would become blue all over, so blue is all that you see from Miramar that it could not be more so, for it is all blue, the blue of the sea and the blue of the sky.

Miramar and most of the neighbouring lands were bought bit by bit by the Archduke Louis Salvador of Austria, who loved and exalted the land in which Ramón Llull had lived. Enchanted one day with these landscapes, he took root in Majorca and, choosing it for his lifelong holiday, converted his possessions into living museums filled with peasant hand work and Majorcan taste.

The road passes through Son Masroig, through Deyá and Lluch Alcarí before arriving at the town of Sóller. This little town, lying in one of the broadest valleys in Majorca, is backed by the Puig Mayor (4741 ft.), the highest mountain in the Island. Lemons, oranges and pomegranates grow in the valley, and you will know when you are getting near Sóller, for you will be struck with the perfume of the orange blossom.

The town is clean and pretty, with white houses and many cool interior courtyards filled with flowers. Like all the small houses in the Majorcan villages, they shine with cleanliness. But Sóller, which has no sea, is above all, the valley of orange trees, — a marvellous orchard.

To go to the sea, Sóller has an old tram that, after toddling along about $3\frac{1}{2}$ miles, comes to its port, which, like Palma, is in a bay, but smaller and closed in.

«Ses Animes» - Tribune

«With a sloping bank, a garland of houses, a pine-cov-
ered hillock and a wall of lofty craggy mountains to shelter the bay from all winds, they have built the most peaceful harbour that the skipper of a sailing boat could hope
to find to retire to», says Rusiñol. Now he would have to
add many hotels and beaches always crowded with bath-

Valldemossa. The Carthusian Monastery.

The Pleyal piano that Chopin had sent direct from Paris.
In the foreground a bust of Chopin by the sculptor J. Borrel Nicolau.

Majorcan piano used by Chopin during his stay in the Cartuja.

The "Sa Foradada" cove.

ers, which does not take away either the quiet or the beauty, but adds to the colour.

From the port of Sóller, excursions can be made by sea to Sa Calobra and to the Torrente de Pareis; others along the coast, following the daring and wonderful track of the new road that goes from Sóller to Lluch. The enthusiastic excursionist finds himself here confronted with the most fantastic trip the Island has to offer him. Going up the road, with its broad and well designed bends, he goes on climbing towards the heights of Puig Mayor. The view over the cockle-shell harbour is a pure delight. After crossing the mountainous wall through a long tunnel, the descent begins.

From the beach, a path and a little tunnel pierced in the

Puig Major

Monasteri de Lluc

Gorg Blau

Torrent de Pareis

Sa Calobra

Mirador de Ses Barques

Fornalutx

Port de Soller

Cap Gros

Sóller

A Palma

Llucalcari

Deià

Son Marroig

Sa Foradada

A Andratx

Valldemossa

A Palma

The Deia cove.

Deia.

Port de Soller

Port de Soller

living rock lead the excursionist to the Pareis torrent, along the bed of which he will arrive, after several hours painful climbing, at Gorg Blau, where the gigantic pass ends.

Going up the road again and turning towards the valley with our back to the sea, we reach a place where the road branches off in two directions, the one on the left going to Lluch

Port de Soller: viewed from «Ses Barques» - Tribune

Torrente de Pareis

The Sanctuary of the Virgin of Lluch, the patron saint of the Majorcans, is the centre and motive of their pilgrimages. It stands at a height of 1311 ft. and is about 11 miles from the important town of Inca, in a very fertile valley clothed in forest and surrounded by mountains. One might say that all roads lead to Lluch from any part of the Island, and those that lead to the Monastery are the most suggestive that the interior can offer the traveler.

**Beach and Mouth of Torrente de Pareis**

On the Sa Calobra Road. «Cavall Bernat»

Road to
Sa Calobra

Sa Calobra

«Torrente de Pareis»

On the Sa Calobra Road. «Nudo de la Corbata»

Sanctuary of the Virgin of Lluc.

In the North of the Island, before reaching Pollensa, it is worth while turning off to San Vicente Cove, near the King's castle, the ruins of which crown the coastal range. Painters, writers and poets have made it known as one of the beauty spots of the Island where — even today — the country is filled with silence. The anchorage opens between steep coasts like a splendid shelter and ends in the spiked crest of the Punta de la Troneta. The roads giving acces to it are easy, whether by land or by sea, and in

Campanet Caves.

Cala Sant Vicenç

front of its intensely blue and transparent waters, some hotels and chalets have already sprung up, that do not alter but rather enhance the impressive beauty of the landscape.

The route from Pollensa to Formentor, the Island's green pearl, runs round the little peninsula of broken rocks. Here and there, where the country seems to widen out to embrace more sea and more land, belvederes have been opened so that those who have come so far and

Pollença . Old Roman Bridge

«Morro d'en Boqué»

«Es Colomé»

expect that, after all that they have seen, there will be
nothing more surprising to see, will find there is still some-
thing more for them to admire. They have before their
eyes coasts, reefs, high mountains, old coastal walls flanked

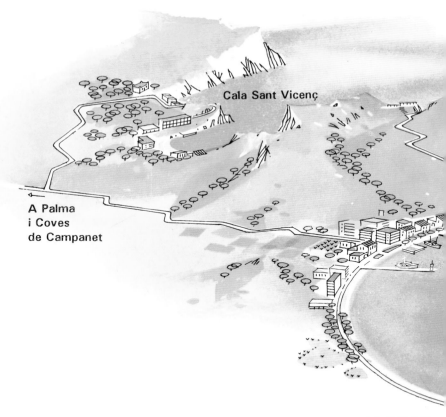

Cala Sant Vicenç

A Palma
i Coves
de Campanet

Formentor

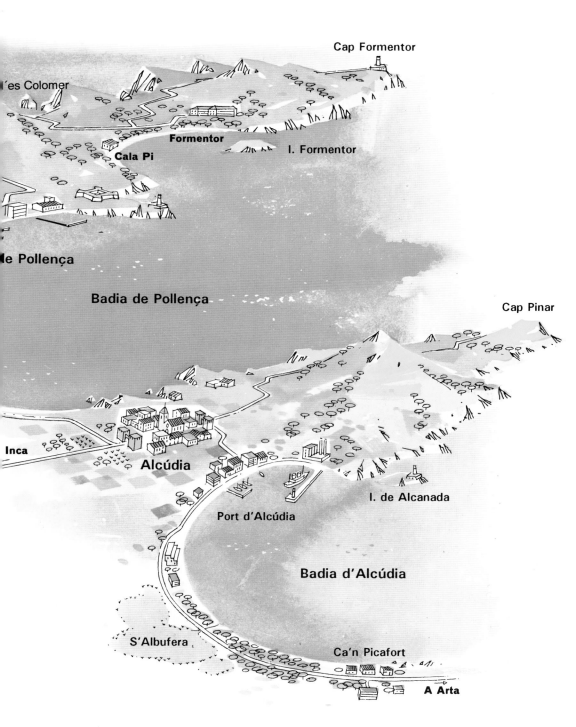

Cap Formentor

´es Colomer

Formentor

Cala Pi

I. Formentor

le Pollença

Badia de Pollença

Cap Pinar

Inca

Alcúdia

I. de Alcanada

Port d'Alcúdia

Badia d'Alcúdia

S'Albufera

Ca'n Picafort

A Arta

Cala Figuera de Formentor

by creeks; and, emerging from the cobalt sea, the islet Es Calomer, in front of the Puig Rock.

Formentor Bay is in itself one of the great attractions of Majorca. The mountains keep watch over it, and the pine forests come down to the very edge of the beach, with their opulent and densely-leaved tops. In Winter it is as warm and mild as in Summer, and the climate and landscape together make it a favoured spot whose existence only seems possible in one's imagination.

In the place called «Pi de la Posada», opposite the island of Formentor, there arose, in 1930, the Hotel Formentor, surrounded by 4940 acres of timber. Among its visitors it can count famous artists, celebrated authors, and statesmen, such as Sir Winston Churchill and the Negus of Abyssinia. The great Majorcan poet Costa y Llobera, who sang of them and extolled them in his writings, is intimately linked with these places.

Formentor is the first sheltered roadstead in the great bay of Pollensa, which we shall now go round to get, once we have passed the Fortaleza (the Fortress), to Pollensa harbour, one of the first residential centres that arose in the Island, and the best known to foreign artists. In the immense anchorage some of the largest squadrons in the

Formentor.

Formentor. Lighthouse

Port de Pollença

Port de Pollença. **Nightfall**

Pollença. Typical Street

Alcudia. City Wall

Can Picafort

world have lain at anchor, and in this delicious settlement there live men from all the continents who, like the great painter Anglada Camarasa, are in love with these landscapes and this calm.

The town of Pollensa, like that of Sóller, is situated towards the interior and is at some 4 or 5 miles from the sea. The country abounds in fertile orchards and is overlorded by the majestic Mount Puig which, with its Sanctuary, con-

Ca'n Picafort

Cala Ratjada

stitutes a lookout over the district. The beauty of Pollensa becomes more solemn at the place called «El Calvario», flanked by cypresses and bathed in a serene and gentle peace.

Alcudia, an old and noble townlet, loved and won by the peoples of ancient times, lies between two bays. On

Cala Ratjada

Capdepera.
The Castle

Entrance to the Caves

Cala Bona

Cala Millor

Cala Millor

Sa Coma. Cala Millor

Sa Coma - S'Illot

its left is Pollensa Bay that we have just left. On the right there is the immense bay that bears the same name as the town. The City has preserved all its fortified gates, remains of walls, and a Greco-Roman theatre beside the harbour.

The vast curve of the Bay shelters the beaches and the modernized parts of Can Picafort, the colony of Son Serra, Cala Guyá, and farther on, already on the South coast, the fortified city of Cap Depera and the famous beaches of Ratjada.

The water that embraces Majorca on the outside, by flowing around inside it for thousands of centuries, too, has carved marvellous sculptures and architectural forms, hollowing it out into vast halls and chambers, in deep curves and magic decorations.

At some 6 miles from the townlet of Artá there are the caves of that name. They are the most grandiose and impressive of the more than 200 discovered in the Island.

Near to Manacor is the entrance to the caves of the Drach. It would be difficult to compare them, as owing to their proportions and nature, any comparison would be impossible. What is immense in Artá is delicate in the Drach. What in the former would be arches decorated with marvels of sculpture on the scale of a great cathedral, would in the latter be the same marvels, but adorning the interior of an enchanted cave. Reliefs and fanciful shapes stress today their beauty illuminated and sonorized (light and sound) by the art of Buigas, the poet of lights, and in the boat trips on the interior lakes the reliefs acquire, with different colours, the fantastic realism of a tale of magic. We should also mention for their spectacular nature the caves of Campanet, on the road from Pollensa to Palma, and those of Llams, near Porto-Cristo.

Manacor, in the interior, is an important townlet domina-

Porto Cristo

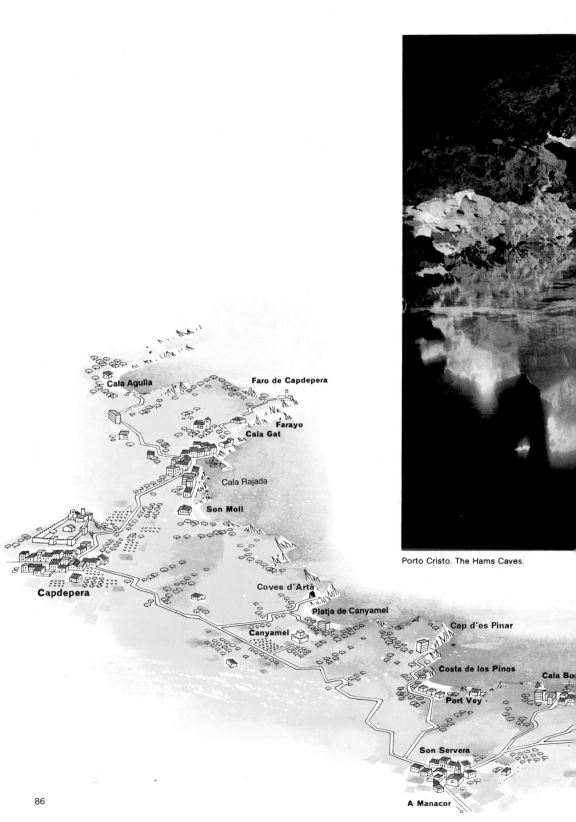

Cala Agulla

Faro de Capdepera

Farayo

Cala Gat

Cala Rajada

Son Moll

Capdepera

Coves d'Artà

Platja de Canyamel

Cap d'es Pinar

Canyamel

Costa de los Pinos

Cala Bo

Port Vey

Son Servera

A Manacor

Porto Cristo. The Hams Caves.

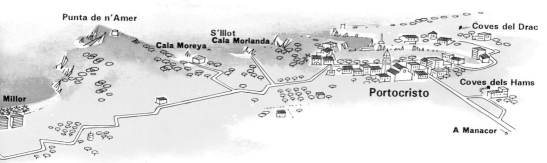

Punta de n'Amer

Cala Moreya

S'Illot
Cala Morlanda

Coves del Drac

Millor

Portocristo

Coves dels Hams

A Manacor

ted by an imposing Gothic cathedral. It has become famous
for its industry — formerly carried on in the houses — in
the manufacture of pearls. At Porto-Cristo the sea runs
well into the land and forms a natural harbour and makes
beaches in front of which hotéls and modern improvements
have sprung up. The feast days are enlivened by the soft
drone of the bagpipes — the «goatsack» — played by a Majorcan attired in the typical dress of the Islanders of the
XVIII century.

Various views of Porto Cristo.

Cala Estany - Playa Romántica

All along the coast facing the sun, creek follows creek, with beaches and tiny harbours. Hotels and modernizations are multiplying wherever they can be assimilated into the landscape that hides them among foliage, thus keeping the natural element intact. After Porto-Cristo there follow

Cala Murada

in order the coves of Aguilar, Mendia, Falcó, Vacas, Mangraner, Barquetas, Bota, Domingo, and Murada. Between Cala Algar and Cala Marsal we find Porto-Colom, a shelter for small boats in the waters of what is already the Felanitx marine front.

Cala Llonga

Porto Colom

Cala d'Or

Sometimes the creek is so deep that the sea, running well inland, is transformed into an intensely blue river. Cala d'Or, the prettiest of them all, with its houses in Ibiza style, is one such case. At its sides, new beaches and new coves are formed, as at Cala Arsenau, Cala Ferrera, Cala Mitjana, Cala Esmeralda, Cala Gran, Cala Llonga — the lake of Cala d'Or —, Porto-Petro, Cala Mondragó...

The centre of the new coastal fringe will now be Santanyi, where the road turns off to go to the Coves of Figuera, Mármol, Socarrada, Llombarts, and Almunia. At Cala Santanyi, at the foot of Terra Nova, stands a gigantic rock, bored into the shape of an arch, known as Es Pontás, which was immortalized by the painter Francisco Fernaressi. The coast continues to Cape Salinas, cut into cliffs and perforated by the entrances to numerous resonant caves. Then come reefs and lofty cliffs as far as the tip of

Cala d'Or

Porto-Petro

Cala Mondragó

Cala Figuera. Caló d'en Boira

Santanyí. «Es Pontás»

A Palma

Santan

Cala Santanyí

Es Pontás

the Cape, from whose lighthouse, lost in the midst of so much sea, but very beautiful sea, one gets a sight of Cabrera, the solitary island.

In a land of so much beauty, the normal passes unnoticed, and so the South coast that brings us back to Palma lives its quiet life, little disturbed by tourists since, though pretty, it is not so strikingly beautiful as the rest. In the

Cala Murada

A Felanitx

Cala Algar

Portocolom

Punta de ses Crestes

Cala Marçal

Cala Mitjana

Calonge

Cala Gran

Cala Esmeralda

Cala d'Or

Cala Llonga

Alquería Blanca

Portopetro

Cala Mondragó

Cala Figuera

Cala Figuera

Cala Figuera - Caló d'en Busques

Cala S'Almonia

interior, too, men and women, attending calmy to their very fertile soil, know little of hotels and motor cars, and go on being land workers and hand workers whilst the sails of their windmills go on leisurely turning.

In the plain there is Petra, famous as the home of Fray Juniper Serra, founder of Los Angeles and evangelizer of California. Inca, in the North, known for its fabulous cellars with their immense vats; Benisalem, which produces the best wines in the Island; Consell, Marratixi, Sancelles, Santa Eugenia, San Juan, Selva — which jealously guards the treasure of its popular dances —, and Randa, in whose Oratory Ramón Llull meditated and wrote his Ars Magna.

Cala Santanyí

Cala Llombards

Such is the beauty of Majorca, the land of old olives and aromatic oranges, — a mixture of ever-moving tourists and amorous calm, a Paradise of poets and nobles.

Santiago Rusiñol, who had the gift of saying things şo well, said of the Island that the greatest laziness that one felt in Majorca was a laziness to leave it.

Colonia Sant Jordi